TrueU: Who Is Jesus?

Copyright © 2013 Focus on the Family. A production of Focus on the Family. All rights reserved. International copyright secured.

A Focus on the Family book published by Tyndale House Publishers, Inc., Carol Stream, Illinois 60188

Focus on the Family and the accompanying logo and design are federally registered trademarks of Focus on the Family, Colorado Springs, CO 80995.

TrueU is a trademark of Focus on the Family.

TYNDALE and Tyndale's quill logo are registered trademarks of Tyndale House Publishers, Inc.

Editor: Ray Seldomridge

Designer: Michael Harrigan

ISBN: 978-1-58997-725-9

Printed in the United States of America

1 2 3 4 5 6 7 8 9 / 19 18 17 16 15 14 13

WHO IS
JESUS?

LESSON 1

THE QUESTION

Who is Jesus Christ? The answer to this question matters more than anything else in the world. But the traditional response, derived from the Gospel accounts, is often deeply offensive to unbelievers.

So despite a solid historical record, many attempts have been made over the centuries to reinvent Jesus and make Him less threatening.

QUOTE UNQUOTE

What did the speaker say? Fill in the blanks as you watch the presentation.

1. The third great truth is _____.

2. Jesus is _____.

3. There will be people who will _____ today because they declared that this Jesus was more than just a man.

4. The Book of Acts ends with _____ being under house arrest.

5. It always surprises me when people are dismissive of Jesus of Nazareth because of what they claim is a lack of _____.

6. Jesus was no _____; He knew how to handle himself in tough conversations.

7. The greatest obstacle that we're going to face is not the obstacle from _____; it's the obstacle from _____.

8. Our quest is to know Him and to know His _____ better than we've ever known it before.

NOTES OR QUESTIONS

While watching the video, use these lines to record your thoughts, any facts you want to remember, questions that arise, etc.

_____

_____

_____

_____

_____

_____

_____

_____

_____

_____

_____

_____

_____

_____

_____

_____

_____

_____

_____

WHAT'S THE BIG IDEA?

NOT MY JESUS!

Many people over the centuries have been offended by the real Jesus Christ because He doesn't fit what they'd like Him to be.

1. What is it about the evangelical Christian view of Jesus that most offends or bothers unbelievers? Why? How do they go about attacking this Jesus?

_____

_____

_____

_____

_____

2. How would you describe the sort of Jesus that non-Christians you know are more comfortable with? On what basis have they formed their picture of Jesus?

_____

_____

_____

_____

_____

3. What ideas do you have on how you might help people encounter the Jesus who's described in the Gospels?

_____

_____

_____

_____

_____

WHAT'S THE BIG IDEA?

CONVINCING EVIDENCE

The historical record concerning Jesus's life and teachings is specific and extensive, beyond that of most people in antiquity.

1. What could you say to people who claim that the Gospel accounts were just made up or modified by Jesus's followers to make Him appear to be God?

_____

_____

_____

_____

_____

2. Does it matter when Matthew, Mark, Luke, and John were written? Why?

_____

_____

_____

_____

_____

3. Do you really think of Jesus as a historical figure, a man who walked the earth, or does He seem to exist in a sort of fictional, "Bibleland" dimension? Why?

_____

_____

_____

_____

_____

WHAT'S THE BIG IDEA?

HELP OUR UNBELIEF

Not only does the world stumble over Jesus, but so do we who claim to know Him.

1. Is there something Jesus said that you have a problem really believing? If so, what is it and why?

_____

_____

_____

_____

_____

2. Do you have trouble with the idea that Jesus is the only way to God? What makes this teaching hard to accept? (We address this more in lesson 9.)

_____

_____

_____

_____

_____

3. Have you made it your main quest in life to know Jesus personally, and to grow in your relationship with Him over time? If so, how are you coming with that? If not, what else seems more important to you?

_____

_____

_____

_____

WHAT DO YOU SAY TO THIS?

Discuss as a group what you would say if a friend, relative, or professor made the following claim:

The early church literally stole Jesus from His original followers, hijacking His human message, shrouding it in an impenetrable cloak of divinity, and using it to expand their own power.

(A quotation from Dan Brown's *The Da Vinci Code*)

Support or add to one another's responses, bringing in any relevant Bible passages. Perhaps you'd even like to role-play the conversation..

WHO IS JESUS?

"Blessed is the one who is not offended by me."
—Matthew 11:6

Jesus—the Jesus we might discover if we really looked!—is larger, more disturbing, more urgent than we—than the church!—had ever imagined.

—N. T. Wright, *Simply Jesus*

The Lord Jesus Christ is far beyond what most of us could ever dream or imagine. His greatness, His beauty, and His splendor are unknown to many Christians today.

—Leonard Sweet and Frank Viola, *Jesus Manifesto*

02

LESSON 2
THE PROMISE

Does it matter that Jesus was Jewish and, more specifically, a "son of David"? Why is His family line important?

The answer goes all the way back to a promise made at the beginning of time. For as soon as Adam and Eve sinned, God said that a descendant of theirs would come to make the world right again.

QUOTE UNQUOTE

What did the speaker say? Fill in the blanks as you watch the presentation.

1. If the Bible speaks to my heart and tells me that Jesus is the
   __messiah__, well that's a whole different story.

2. The promises to Abraham and to David weren't promises about
   __camels__ and __sheep__.

3. People were crying out hosanna to the son of David. Why is all
   of this stuff focused upon a __genealogy__?

4. "You will strike his heel, but he will crush your head." This is a
   very __mysterious__ promise.

5. Now, this is not your __pristine__ family tree.

6. He [Jesus] had to be within a __specific__
   family, a __specific__ tribe, a
   __specific__ nation that was part of the road
   map that God gave to the Jewish people.

7. So we have the gospel, the good news, preached back in the
   __garden__.

NOTES OR QUESTIONS

While watching the video, use these lines to record your thoughts, any facts you want to remember, questions that arise, etc.

_____

_____

_____

_____

_____

_____

_____

_____

_____

_____

_____

_____

_____

_____

_____

_____

_____

_____

_____

_____

WHAT'S THE BIG IDEA?

DECLARATION OF WAR

In the Garden of Eden, God promised that the "seed of the woman" would eventually crush Satan and make the world right again.

1. Did you realize that the gospel was, in cryptic terms, already being proclaimed immediately after the Fall? What does that tell you about our Lord?

_____

_____

_____

_____

_____

_____

_____

_____

2. Has God's promise been fulfilled? What evidence do you base your answer on?

Yes. The Bible.

_____

_____

_____

_____

_____

_____

_____

_____

WHAT'S THE BIG IDEA?

FOLLOW THE LINE

The Bible traces Eve's descendants all the way to Abraham, who heard the promise anew, and then on to David, from whose line the Messiah, the "son of David," would come.

1. Have you ever paid much attention to Jesus's genealogy, or has it seemed too boring and beside the point? Explain in your own words why it's in the Bible.

It's there to prove that Jesus is the promised messiah.

2. How important is the Old Testament in our quest to understand who Jesus is? Do you sometimes tend to read only the New Testament? Why?

3. What do you think of the differences in Jesus's genealogy that appear in Matthew and Luke? And what do you conclude from the fact that many of Jesus's ancestors were less than reputable?

WHAT'S THE BIG IDEA?

THE PROMISED MESSIAH

After centuries of silence, Jesus came to earth, showing by His lineage that He was the foretold son of David who would fulfill God's promise by dying for the whole world.

1. How might you view reality if the Messiah had never come? Try to imagine or recall your life without God. Have you come to take Jesus for granted?

_____

_____

_____

_____

_____

_____

_____

_____

2. Has the Messiah's mission been accomplished? If not, describe in broad terms what all of God's work is still leading up to. Has He given up on what He started in the Garden of Eden?

_____

_____

_____

_____

_____

_____

_____

_____

WHAT DO YOU SAY TO THIS?

Discuss as a group what you would say if a friend, relative, or professor drew the following conclusion:

The Gospels . . . are meant to declare religious truths, not historical facts.

(A quotation from Bart Ehrman, professor at University of North Carolina, in *Newsweek*, Dec. 10, 2012)

Support or add to one another's responses, bringing in any relevant Bible passages. Perhaps you'd even like to role-play the conversation..

WHO IS JESUS?

"I am the root and the descendant of David, the bright morning star."

—Revelation 22:16

For far too long now Christians have told the story of Jesus as if it hooked up not with the story of Israel, but simply with the story of human sin as in Genesis 3, skipping over the story of Israel altogether.

—N. T. Wright, *How God Became King*

Jesus said to them, "Truly, truly, I say to you, before Abraham was, I am."

—John 8:58

03

LESSON 3
THE PROPHECY

God didn't just make a promise to mankind once and then drop it. Over many centuries, He raised up numerous prophets who reiterated His plan to rescue His people through a Messiah.

Some of the those prophecies were very specific, making it unlikely that anyone could fulfill all of them. But someone did.

QUOTE UNQUOTE

What did the speaker say? Fill in the blanks as you watch the presentation.

1. There is a lot of debate about how many prophecies exist . . .
   that point to Jesus; conservatively some people will say there
   are _____ or so.

2. Isaiah _____53_____ has always been looked upon
   traditionally as pointing to the Messiah.

3. We live in a culture that's very ___skeptical___ about
   prophecies.

4. They believed that God was the one who was
   _____ through all of history.

5. It's not an evidential problem. . . . It's a _____
   problem; it's a _____ problem.

6. This is the ___Kairos___ moment that all of history was
   waiting for.

7. It's been ___400___ years; we haven't heard anything
   from God.

8. In the ___fullness___ of time, the right time, God
   brought forth His son born of a woman and fulfilled all the
   promises and all the prophecies.

NOTES OR QUESTIONS

While watching the video, use these lines to record your thoughts, any facts you want to remember, questions that arise, etc.

_____

_____

_____

_____

_____

_____

_____

_____

_____

_____

_____

_____

_____

_____

_____

_____

_____

_____

_____

_____

_____

WHAT'S THE BIG IDEA?

A DELIVERER

The expected coming of a Messiah was the main theme of all the Old Testament prophecies and the longing of every Jew in Jesus's day.

1. What did these prophecies have to do with God's earlier promises—in the Garden, and to Abraham and David?

_____

_____

_____

_____

_____

_____

_____

2. Imagine that you were living in Jesus's day. Honestly, what might you have thought of this man from Nazareth? Do you think you would have been a follower or a sceptic? What sort of Messiah would you have been looking for?

_____

_____

_____

_____

_____

_____

_____

_____

WHAT'S THE BIG IDEA?

WE HAVE A MATCH

Against astronomical odds, Jesus fulfilled all the various and detailed prophecies about the Messiah, even though most of these were outside His control.

1. By "outside His control," Del meant that Jesus couldn't just read
   about something in the Scriptures and then go act accordingly
   to make it come true. Identify some prophecies that were
   beyond His control.

_____

_____

_____

_____

_____

_____

_____

_____

2. Do the odds impress you, or do you tend to downplay the Old
   Testament prophecies as evidence of God's involvement?
   Why?

_____

_____

_____

_____

_____

_____

_____

_____

WHAT'S THE BIG IDEA?

THE SILENCE WAS BROKEN

For 400 years, God did not speak to His chosen people. But then, at just the right time, all the promises and prophecies about the Messiah came true in the person of Jesus.

1. Are you surprised by Luke's statement that "beginning with Moses
   and all the Prophets, he [Jesus] interpreted to them in all the
   Scriptures the things concerning himself" (24:27)? Where might
   you find some of the Old Testament prophecies that Jesus
   fulfilled?

_____

_____

_____

_____

_____

_____

_____

2. It's been over 2,000 years since Jesus came; does it feel to you
   as if God has gone silent again? What promises or prophecies
   has God made about our future with Jesus that you really cling
   to? Or do you not think much about life beyond this present one?
   Why?

_____

_____

_____

_____

_____

_____

_____

WHAT DO YOU SAY TO THIS?

Discuss as a group what you would say if a friend, relative, or professor made the following statement:

I'm not Jewish, so I'm not looking for any sort of Messiah, and I don't care about some old Jewish writings from eons ago.

Support or add to one another's responses, bringing in any relevant Bible passages. Perhaps you'd even like to role-play the conversation..

WHO IS JESUS?

His name shall be called Wonderful Counselor, Mighty God, Everlasting Father, Prince of Peace. Of the increase of his government and of peace there will be no end.

—Isaiah 9:6-7

Surely he has borne our griefs and carried our sorrows; yet we esteemed him stricken, smitten by God, and afflicted. But he was wounded for our transgressions; he was crushed for our iniquities; upon him was the chastisement that brought us peace, and with his stripes we are healed.

—Isaiah 53:4-5

LESSON 4
HIS LIFE

What was Jesus like? What sort of things did He say and do? How did He treat the people around Him?

Nearly everyone has some vague ideas about who Jesus was. But often that mental picture doesn't match what the Gospels reveal. Jesus's actions, His words, and His penetrating encounters with other people were nothing less than shocking.

QUOTE UNQUOTE

What did the speaker say? Fill in the blanks as you watch the presentation.

1. He [Jesus] amazed people and He _____ others.

2. There are people who . . . would discount any kind of record that includes something _miraculous_.

3. The miracles of Jesus were primarily to _bear testimony_ that He was who He said He was.

4. All of a sudden His [Jesus's] words were starting to get

   _____.

5. The Sadducees, remember, they take their shot at Jesus, trying to trip Him up as well, and Jesus left them _speechless_.

6. We encounter a person . . . who stands out from

   _____ _____, who is compelling

   by the substance of His teaching and by the manner of His

   character.

7. The words of Jesus were _astonishing_ in His

   day, and they are still _astonishing_ in our day.

8. People are making a lot of money off of trying to

   debunk Jesus.

9. This is a spiritual battle that we're fighting; it's not an

   _____ one.

NOTES OR QUESTIONS

•••••

While watching the video, use these lines to record your thoughts, any facts you want to remember, questions that arise, etc.

~~Jesus~~ Jesus said to forgive, love, and turn the other cheek.

WHAT'S THE BIG IDEA?

TRUTH DEMONSTRATED

Jesus's miracles provided important evidence that He really was who He said He was.

1. Why else did Jesus do miracles? Why did He heal people, and how can you know?

_____

_____

_____

_____

_____

_____

_____

_____

2. Seriously, turning water into wine? Walking on water? Calming a storm? Do you really believe that Jesus did such things? Or do you suspect that these events were blown out of proportion in a non-scientific age?

_____

_____

_____

_____

_____

_____

_____

_____

WHAT'S THE BIG IDEA?

SHOCKING WORDS

Jesus's words are bold, fearless, authoritative— even astonishing. They are often extremely discomforting, even to believers.

1. What are some ways that unbelievers respond to a saying from Jesus that they don't like or agree with? What sort of things did He say that bother them most?

_____

_____

_____

_____

_____

2. Identify some things Jesus said that really bother or worry you. How do you respond to words that make you feel guilty?

_____

_____

_____

_____

_____

3. What are some things Jesus said that go way over your head? That you just can't grasp the meaning of?

_____

_____

_____

_____

_____

WHAT'S THE BIG IDEA?

THIS IS ETERNAL LIFE . . .

To know Jesus, and to become deeply immersed in every aspect of His teaching, His works, and His character, should be the primary quest of our lives.

1. Do the Christians you know seem to be more captivated by Jesus than by anything else? If not, what takes their everyday attention?

_____

_____

_____

_____

_____

2. What about you? Have you read the Gospels so many times that it feels as though there's nothing more to learn about Jesus? Does He intrigue you very much? Why or why not?

_____

_____

_____

_____

_____

3. What is one of the best ways to get to know Jesus better? (For a hint, read John 14:21.)

_____

_____

_____

_____

_____

WHAT DO YOU SAY TO THIS?

Discuss as a group what you would say if a friend, relative, or professor made the following statement:

I have no use for organized religion or any kind of church, but I think Jesus himself was a good person. He's cool.

Support or add to one another's responses, bringing in any relevant Bible passages. Perhaps you'd even like to role-play the conversation..

WHO IS JESUS?

They were astonished, and said, "Where did this man get this wisdom and these mighty works? Is not this the carpenter's son?"

—Matthew 13:54-55

We have seen his glory, glory as of the only Son from the Father, full of grace and truth. .

—John 1:14

The figure in the Gospels does indeed utter in words of almost heart-breaking beauty his pity for our broken hearts. But they are very far from being the only sort of words that he utters.

—G. K. Chesterton, *The Everlasting Man*

05

LESSON 5

THE DEATH

It's a fact: Jesus died on a cross. But why? What did it mean? And how is His death central to our life?

First, Del helps us relive in detail the events of Jesus's last week. Then he explores the unseen realities that made the Crucifixion necessary.

QUOTE UNQUOTE

What did the speaker say? Fill in the blanks as you watch the presentation.

1. "For this reason I was born, and for this I came into the world, to

_____ _____ _____ _____."

2. Jesus said He came to give His life as a _____.

3. Jesus is the one who changed the _____.

4. Peter actually took Jesus aside, because you don't want to take

someone to the _____ in front of other

people.

5. I can imagine when the disciples heard the word

_____ , their blood probably ran cold.

6. The Romans were very adept at _____.

7. Josephus called it [crucifixion] "the most

_____ of deaths."

8. Even atheist scholars recognize the _____

of Christ [as] being historical.

NOTES OR QUESTIONS

While watching the video, use these lines to record your thoughts, any facts you want to remember, questions that arise, etc.

_____

_____

_____

_____

_____

_____

_____

_____

_____

_____

_____

_____

_____

_____

_____

_____

_____

_____

_____

_____

WHAT'S THE BIG IDEA?

BORN TO DIE

Jesus told His disciples that His reason for coming to earth was to die in our place, which is why the Gospels deal mostly with the last three days of Jesus's life.

1. How did it affect you to hear Del recount in detail what happened at the end of Jesus's life?

_____

_____

_____

_____

_____

_____

_____

_____

2. Why was Jesus's death necessary for our salvation? Couldn't God just forgive our sins without having Christ die?

_____

_____

_____

_____

_____

_____

_____

_____

_____

WHAT'S THE BIG IDEA?

A MATTER OF FACT

The execution of Jesus on a Roman cross is widely viewed as a historical fact even by critical and atheistic scholars.

1. Why did Jesus's death have to be so cruel and barbaric? What difference does it make to know the physical pain He endured?

_____

_____

_____

_____

_____

_____

_____

_____

2. How does celebrating the Lord's Supper help you "proclaim" and remember His death until He comes again?

_____

_____

_____

_____

_____

_____

_____

_____

_____

WHAT'S THE BIG IDEA?

ONE FOR ALL

What matters most about the crucifixion of Jesus is not the physical details, but rather the unseen realities—the reason He died, and how His death saved us.

1. Do you really sense that Jesus died for *you*, not just for others?

_____

_____

_____

_____

_____

_____

_____

_____

_____

2. The New Testament says we should expect to share in Jesus's
   sufferings. What might that mean, and are you prepared to do
   that?

_____

_____

_____

_____

_____

_____

_____

_____

_____

WHAT DO YOU SAY TO THIS?

Discuss as a group what you would say if a friend, relative, or professor made the following statement:

You Christians have some strange ideas about God. How can someone's death serve as a "ransom" or "atonement" to save others?

Support or add to one another's responses, bringing in any relevant Bible passages. Perhaps you'd even like to role-play the conversation..

WHO IS JESUS?

He humbled himself by becoming obedient to the point of death, even death on a cross. Therefore God has highly exalted him and bestowed on him the name that is above every name.

—Philippians 2:8-9

You, who once were alienated and hostile in mind, doing evil deeds, he has now reconciled in his body of flesh by his death, in order to present you holy and blameless and above reproach before him.

—Colossians 1:21-22

06

LESSON 6

THE
RESURRECTION

Dead people don't usually return to life. Even 2,000 years ago, everyone knew that. So when a crucified Jesus reappeared to His disciples, it changed everything—for them and for us.

In this lecture, we learn what attempts have been made to explain away the historical reality of Jesus's resurrection. Then we consider where we'd be without it.

QUOTE UNQUOTE

What did the speaker say? Fill in the blanks as you watch the presentation.

1. Jesus really died, but it was the _____ of Jesus that was appearing to people.

2. Hallucinations are usually a very individual kind of a thing.

3. Somewhere between the time He was put in the tomb and Sunday morning, Jesus revived.

4. There is no inconsistency in the story of the burial of Jesus.

5. Over time, a legend begins to be formed about Jesus, and it just gets embellished, year after year.

6. I think one of the greatest bits of evidence for the Resurrection is the changed lives of His disciples.

7. A legend requires at least two full generations before it can begin to be formed.

8. If Jesus really didn't rise from the dead, then the gospel is useless.

9. How many people will die for a lie when they know it's a lie?

NOTES OR QUESTIONS

While watching the video, use these lines to record your thoughts, any facts you want to remember, questions that arise, etc.

_____

_____

_____

_____

_____

_____

_____

_____

_____

_____

_____

_____

_____

_____

_____

_____

_____

_____

_____

_____

WHAT'S THE BIG IDEA?

JESUS RAISED, ARGUMENTS RAISED

Despite all the physical evidence, many arguments have been advanced against the idea that Jesus rose from the dead.

1. Which of the theories against the Resurrection, if any, do you encounter most often? What is your best argument against it?

_____

_____

_____

2. Do you sense that people who want to argue about the Resurrection are actually interested in looking at the evidence? What's their motivation?

_____

_____

_____

3. Do you know anyone who became a Christian after being convinced of the evidence surrounding the Resurrection? Is this rare today? Why or why not?

_____

_____

_____

4. What might you say to the person who thinks that all this evidence regarding Jesus and His resurrection is just "religious stuff for Christians" but of no interest to anyone else? In other words, what if he or she has no knowledge of the Bible or desire to look into it?

_____

_____

_____

WHAT'S THE BIG IDEA?

EVERYTHING DEPENDS ON THE EMPTY TOMB

If Jesus had not risen from the dead, then Christianity, and our entire biblical worldview, would have been proved false.

1. Explain in your own words how the Resurrection is the key to our faith, and without it, nothing we believe is likely to be true.

_____

_____

_____

2. Some people who consider themselves Christians nonetheless discount the Resurrection. How can this be? Explain.

_____

_____

_____

3. How do you feel about the fact that you, too, will someday undergo resurrection and will live forever in a physical body? Do you recognize this truth from the Bible, or have you been more influenced by the Greek notion that eternal life is somehow "spiritual" (by which you mean nonphysical)?

_____

_____

_____

4. What does the Bible say about the future resurrection or renewal of the entire creation, not just of individual Christians?

_____

_____

_____

WHAT DO YOU SAY TO THIS?

Discuss as a group what you would say if a friend, relative, or professor made the following claim:

The meanings of the Easter stories in the Gospels and the affirmation of Jesus's resurrection in the rest of the New Testament are . . . not dependent upon whether a spectacular miracle happened to the physical body of Jesus.

(A quotation from Marcus Borg on his website, marcusjborg.com, 4/13/12)

Support or add to one another's responses, bringing in any relevant Bible passages. Perhaps you'd even like to role-play the conversation..

WHO IS JESUS?

"I am the first and the last, and the living one. I died, and behold I am alive forevermore, and I have the keys of Death and Hades."

—Revelation 1:17-18

He raised him from the dead and seated him at his right hand in the heavenly places, far above all rule and authority and power and dominion, and above every name that is named, not only in this age but also in the one to come.

—Ephesians 1:20-21

07

LESSON 7

THE "GOD" CLAIM

Don't you love those silly disciples of Jesus, who got carried away and started claiming that their leader was God? But wait, it seems Jesus himself left a lot of clues that would make one suspect He was no ordinary guy.

In this session, we weigh the arguments traditionally made against Jesus's divinity and then start to look at all the evidence in favor of it.

QUOTE UNQUOTE

What did the speaker say? Fill in the blanks as you watch the presentation.

1. If Jesus is God, then everything begins to _____ _____.

2. If Jesus is really God, then the _____ are huge.

3. He [Jesus] acted as if He could actually _____ the sins of people.

4. I can't think of another human being whose reputation was actually _____, the closer that you peered into their life.

5. Jesus accepted _____.

6. If He was either delusional or a deceiver or even a nice deceiver, you couldn't call Him a _____ _____.

7. Jesus taught and spoke with _____ authority.

8. Jesus is either Almighty God or He is _____ beyond belief.

NOTES OR QUESTIONS

While watching the video, use these lines to record your thoughts,
any facts you want to remember, questions that arise, etc.

_____

_____

_____

_____

_____

_____

_____

_____

_____

_____

_____

_____

_____

_____

_____

_____

_____

_____

_____

_____

WHAT'S THE BIG IDEA?

GOD BECAME MAN

If Jesus is really God, the consequences are beyond measure.

1. What are some of those consequences? Talk about it. What does this tell us about God, and what does it tell us about man?

_____

_____

_____

_____

_____

2. Does it strike you as strange or incredible that the Creator of the universe has become one of us? What other adjectives would you use to describe such an idea?

_____

_____

_____

_____

_____

3. Name a few people from the past who either claimed to be God or were proclaimed by others to be God. What happens when people engage in hero worship?

_____

_____

_____

_____

_____

WHAT'S THE BIG IDEA?

MAYBE JUST A MAN?

Many arguments have been made against Jesus's divinity.

1. What arguments have you heard or read? Based on what evidence or reasoning?

_____

_____

_____

_____

_____

_____

_____

_____

2. If any of your friends or family members or professors used one of these arguments, how would you respond?

_____

_____

_____

_____

_____

_____

_____

_____

_____

WHAT'S THE BIG IDEA?

REASONS TO BELIEVE

The Gospels offer at least seven kinds of evidence for Jesus's divine nature.

1. What evidence of Jesus's divinity do you consider to be most compelling? Why?

_____

_____

_____

_____

_____

_____

_____

2. When did Jesus's disciples come to really understand that He was God? Knowing who He was, can you imagine even being near Him? How would you feel?

_____

_____

_____

_____

_____

_____

_____

_____

Discuss as a group what you would say if a friend, relative, or professor made the following statement:

What does it mean to say that Jesus forgave "sins" and lived a "sinless" life? I'm a good person; I don't think I need God's forgiveness. None of us may be perfect, but how does that make us "sinners"?

Support or add to one another's responses, bringing in any relevant Bible passages. Perhaps you'd even like to role-play the conversation..

WHO IS JESUS?

He is the radiance of the glory of God and the exact imprint of his nature, and he upholds the universe by the word of his power.

—Hebrews 1:3

No atheist or blasphemer believes that the author of the Parable of the Prodigal Son was a monster with one mad idea like a cyclops with one eye.

—G. K. Chesterton, *The Everlasting Man*

Jesus Christ has never been a social activist or a moral philosopher. To pitch Him that way is to drain His glory.

—Leonard Sweet and Frank Viola, *Jesus Manifesto*

08

LESSON 8

THE "GOD" CLAIM II

Even a casual reading of the Gospels blows apart the idea that Jesus's followers turned this kindly teacher into a god of their own invention.

Through a stunning barrage of quotations from Jesus himself, we discover that He spoke as only a mad man—or God himself—could.

QUOTE UNQUOTE

What did the speaker say? Fill in the blanks as you watch the presentation.

1. He spoke as if God were not only His Father, but . . . as if He had this relationship with God that was _____.

2. He called himself the _____ and the
   _____.

3. Jesus calls himself _____ _____ _____. That's no big deal; . . . we're all children of God, correct? No.

4. Son of Man became equated to _____ and
   _____ ___ _____.

5. Jesus was not saying, "I and the Father are the same person." He is saying, "I and the Father are the same thing. We're one in
   _____."

6. They picked up stones to stone Him not because He got His
   _____ wrong.

7. He says, "I am," and all they [the soldiers] can do is
   _____ _____ _____ _____.

8. You and I are called to be witnesses to who Jesus is, and the final proof is the greatest proof, and that's the
   _____.

NOTES OR QUESTIONS

While watching the video, use these lines to record your thoughts,
any facts you want to remember, questions that arise, etc.

_____

_____

_____

_____

_____

_____

_____

_____

_____

_____

_____

_____

_____

_____

_____

_____

_____

_____

_____

_____

WHAT'S THE BIG IDEA?

I STAND WITH MY FATHER

Jesus spoke of His unique relationship with God the Father.

1. Is the very notion of a personal God rejected by many people you know, or do most of them agree that, in one way or another, "there is a God"? What would you say to atheists?

_____

_____

_____

_____

_____

2. Pretend, for the moment, that Jesus was just a man, then read some of the things He said about the Father and test the sound of His words. Could what Jesus said be interpreted to mean nothing more than "I, an ordinary man, feel close to God"? Why or why not?

_____

_____

_____

_____

3. Do you pray to the Father, or to Jesus, or to the Spirit, or to all of them? Why? When? Does it matter?

_____

_____

_____

_____

WHAT'S THE BIG IDEA?

GLIMPSES OF GOD

Jesus displayed characteristics that only God can have.

1. Did Jesus know everything? How do you view the mystery of Jesus being both *fully* God and *fully* man? Do you tend to emphasize one aspect of His nature over the other? Why?

_____

_____

_____

_____

_____

2. If Jesus, being God, never changes (Hebrews 13:8), then He is still a man today. How does that affect your relationship with Him?

_____

_____

_____

_____

3. In your everyday life, what does it mean that "all things were created through him [Jesus] and for him. And he is before all things, and in him all things hold together" (Colossians 1:16-17)?

_____

_____

_____

_____

_____

WHAT'S THE BIG IDEA?

I AM

Using various titles, Jesus clearly claimed to be God.

1. Do you find Jesus's words to be breathtaking, even shocking, or are you so familiar with them that they don't come across that way anymore? How might we see in a fresh way what's really there in the Gospels?

_____

_____

_____

_____

_____

2. Do you grasp why Jesus could only be either a fraud or else God himself? Explain.

_____

_____

_____

_____

3. Can you blame Jesus's enemies, or His disciples, for not really understanding who He was at first? How can anyone come to believe that the Creator of 100 billion galaxies became a mere man?

_____

_____

_____

_____

WHAT DO YOU SAY TO THIS?

Discuss as a group what you would say if a friend, relative, or professor made the following claim:

God the Father, Jesus Christ, and the Holy Ghost are separate beings. . . . One must look to the third- and fourth-century Christian church, not to the New Testament itself, to make a strong case for the Trinity.

(A quotation from Robert L. Millet, former dean of religious education at Brigham Young University, on mormonnewsroom.org)

Support or add to one another's responses, bringing in any relevant Bible passages. Perhaps you'd even like to role-play the conversation..

WHO IS JESUS?

A voice came from heaven, "You are my beloved Son; with you I am well pleased."

—Luke 3:22

"Whoever has seen me has seen the Father."

—John 14:9

He is the image of the invisible God, the firstborn of all creation. For by him all things were created, in heaven and on earth, visible and invisible, whether thrones or dominions or rulers or authorities—all things were created through him and for him. And he is before all things, and in him all things hold together.

—Colossians 1:15-17

09

LESSON 9

IS JESUS
THE ONLY WAY?

Previously we dealt with the big question, "Is Jesus God?" This time, we address the really tough question, "Is Jesus the only way?"

What makes this so hard is that our society loves tolerance and diversity. So when a person comes along and says his way is the only way on some issue, he is labeled a bigot. And honestly, he is one— unless he happens to be right.

QUOTE UNQUOTE

What did the speaker say? Fill in the blanks as you watch the presentation.

1. Is Jesus the only way? _____ may end up asking this more than anybody else.

2. _____ is our best friend. We live in a very "_____" world.

3. If I'm a follower of Jesus, I'm going to say what _____ _____.

4. A lot of people will try to make you the problem; you're the one who's _____.

5. Jesus also declared that any other way was _____.

6. We struggle with exclusivity because we think too _____ of Jesus.

7. A _____ god would be the eternal Alone One.

8. There is no _____ _____ with Jesus.

NOTES OR QUESTIONS

While watching the video, use these lines to record your thoughts, any facts you want to remember, questions that arise, etc.

_____

_____

_____

_____

_____

_____

_____

_____

_____

_____

_____

_____

_____

_____

_____

_____

_____

_____

_____

_____

WHAT'S THE BIG IDEA?

ALL THINGS BEING UNEQUAL

The idea that all religions are the same or are compatible makes no sense when you look at what they actually teach.

1. When people say that all religions are the same, do they even know what the major religions teach? Or are they speaking emotionally, without knowledge? What motivates them to embrace diversity, whether on this issue or another?

_____

_____

_____

_____

_____

2. Do you know enough about other religions like Islam and Buddhism in order to point out the major differences with Christianity? How might you prepare better?

_____

_____

_____

_____

3. Is there any truth in other religions? Explain.

_____

_____

_____

_____

_____

WHAT'S THE BIG IDEA?

TAKE IT UP WITH JESUS

We didn't make Christianity exclusive; Jesus did.

1. Jesus said He was the only way to God. What determines whether He was being arrogant or simply telling the truth?

_____

_____

_____

_____

_____

2. Del says that the question "Is Jesus the only way?" is a hard one for us. How so? Is it hard intellectually? Emotionally? Socially? What makes this issue difficult?

_____

_____

_____

_____

_____

3. If there were many different ways to God, would Jesus have needed to die? Explain.

_____

_____

_____

_____

_____

WHAT'S THE BIG IDEA?

MORE THAN A TEACHER

The real reason for Jesus being the only way to God is that He *is* God, not just a teacher or go-between.

1. Who has the right or authority to determine what paths there are to God? Why?

_____

_____

_____

_____

_____

2. Del said that the higher we see Jesus, the more it makes sense that He is the only way. What did he mean?

_____

_____

_____

_____

3. What if finding God is not so much about what we do to discover Him as it is about what *God* did (on the Cross) to make such a reunion possible? How does this differ from other religions?

_____

_____

_____

_____

_____

WHAT DO YOU SAY TO THIS?

Discuss as a group what you would say if a friend, relative, or professor said the following:

What about a man in the jungle of Africa or Indonesia who has never heard of Jesus? Can he not find God? Will he not be saved?

Support or add to one another's responses, bringing in any relevant Bible passages. Perhaps you'd even like to role-play the conversation..

WHO IS JESUS?

Whoever does not believe is condemned already, because he has not believed in the name of the only Son of God.

—John 3:18

"I am the way, and the truth, and the life. No one comes to the Father except through me."

—John 14:6

"There is salvation in no one else, for there is no other name under heaven given among men by which we must be saved."

—Acts 4:12

There is one God, and there is one mediator between God and men, the man Christ Jesus, who gave himself as a ransom for all.

— 1 Timothy 2:5-6

HANDLING
THE QUESTIONS

In this final session, we consider how best to introduce people to the real Jesus—a Jesus that they may fear more than anything else. The Bible doesn't just tell us about our Lord; it also instructs us on how to represent Him in front of others who haven't met Him.

Often the most effective—even electrifying—way to be a witness for Jesus is to get out of the way and let His own words speak for themselves.

QUOTE UNQUOTE

What did the speaker say? Fill in the blanks as you watch the presentation.

1. We need to _____ _____ _____ Him.

2. All truth flows from the very _____ and
   _____ of God.

3. "Look! You're not listening to me. I _____ Him!"

4. They didn't just believe that Jesus rose from the dead . . . ; they
   were _____.

5. To be effective in persuading people today, we have to do it in
   a _____.

6. Sometimes you can get yourselves into a _____
   situation.

7. _____ what you don't know.

8. _____ before, _____ during, _____ after.

9. We are increasingly a culture of _____.

10. People are _____ of the real Jesus.

NOTES OR QUESTIONS

While watching the video, use these lines to record your thoughts, any facts you want to remember, questions that arise, etc.

_____

_____

_____

_____

_____

_____

_____

_____

_____

_____

_____

_____

_____

_____

_____

_____

_____

_____

_____

_____

WHAT'S THE BIG IDEA?

SHOW THE WAY

It's more important to *handle* people's questions about Jesus than to *answer* them.

1. What does Del mean by this? Do you agree or disagree, and why?

_____

_____

_____

_____

_____

_____

_____

_____

2. What comes before—and is more important than—being a
   witness for Christ? Why? How are you doing with this?

_____

_____

_____

_____

_____

_____

_____

_____

WHAT'S THE BIG IDEA?

PASS IT ON

As Christ's witnesses, we must prepare, persuade, and pray.

1. Describe in your own words what Del means by "pulling people into the story" of Jesus rather than just doling out facts. How can you tell the story with passion? How can you practice telling it?

_____

_____

_____

_____

_____

2. What is the difference between being a faithful witness and an effective witness? What does it mean to "persuade"?

_____

_____

_____

_____

_____

3. Why is it important to develop a relationship with an unbeliever and treat that person with grace and respect?

_____

_____

_____

_____

_____

WHAT'S THE BIG IDEA?

WIN SOME, LOSE SOME

We must expect that often people will be skeptical, apathetic, or afraid of committing their lives to Christ.

1. Is it up to us to bring others to faith in Jesus? How can we know when to "engage in battle" and when to hold our peace?

_____

_____

_____

_____

_____

_____

_____

_____

_____

2. Jesus said, "By this all people will know that you are my disciples, if you have love for one another" (John 13:35). So how can we reach people who are not persuaded by our words?

_____

_____

_____

_____

_____

_____

_____

WHAT DO YOU SAY TO THIS?

Role-play within your group what you would say if a friend, relative, or professor made the following request:

Of course I've heard of Jesus before but never actually read anything about Him. Please tell me the story and explain why He's such an important figure to you.

Support or add to one another's responses, bringing in any relevant Bible passages. Perhaps you'd even like to role-play the conversation..

WHO IS JESUS?

I ask you to look at the Jesus of the Bible. Look at Him. And pray that you will see the self-authenticating glory that is really there. .

—John Piper, sermon on May 20, 2001

I count everything as loss because of the surpassing worth of knowing Christ Jesus my Lord. For his sake I have suffered the loss of all things and count them as rubbish, in order that I may gain Christ and be found in him.

—Philippians 3:8-9

In your hearts honor Christ the Lord as holy, always being prepared to make a defense to anyone who asks you for a reason for the hope that is in you; yet do it with gentleness and respect.

—1 Peter 3:15

Have mercy on those who doubt; save others by snatching them out of the fire.

—Jude 1:22-23

A QUIZ

JESUS'S NATURE

Was Jesus
actually God?
Or was He a man?
Both?
Neither?

QUIZ

Read the following quotations, then for each one, decide whether you agree or disagree. At the end of this quiz, discover the source of each statement.

1. In the fifteenth year of Tiberius Caesar, Pontius Pilate being governor of Judea, Jesus descended [out of heaven] into Capernaum, a city in Galilee, and was teaching on the Sabbath days; And they were astonished at his doctrine.

☐ Agree ☐ Disagree

2. Many deceivers have gone out into the world, those who do not confess the coming of Jesus Christ in the flesh.

☐ Agree ☐ Disagree

3. God created Jesus before he created Adam. . . . Jesus's life began long before he was born in a stable in Bethlehem. . . . As God's firstborn Son, Jesus was a spirit creature in heaven before he was born as a human on earth.

☐ Agree ☐ Disagree

4. In him the whole fullness of deity dwells bodily, and you have been filled in him, who is the head of all rule and authority.

☐ Agree ☐ Disagree

5. We believe in one Lord, Jesus Christ, the only Son of God,

eternally begotten of the Father, God from God, Light from
Light, true God from true God, begotten, not made, of one
Being with the Father. Through him all things were made. . . .

☐ Agree ☐ Disagree

6. The Son is not unbegotten, nor in any way part of the
unbegotten; and . . . He does not derive His subsistence from
any matter. . . . The Son has a beginning, but . . . God is without
beginning. . . .[The Son] is neither part of God, nor of any
essential being.

☐ Agree ☐ Disagree

7. He was conceived by the power of the Holy Spirit and born of
the Virgin Mary. He suffered under Pontius Pilate, was crucified,
died, and was buried. He descended to the dead. On the third
day He rose again. . . .

☐ Agree ☐ Disagree

8. Jesus did not *temporarily* become man, but ... His divine nature
was *permanently* united to His human nature.... Jesus will
remain fully God and fully man, yet one person, forever.

☐ Agree ☐ Disagree

Sources

1. Marcion, The Gospel of Marcion, -AD 140; 2. 2 John 1:7; 3. Jehovah's Witnesses website (jw.
org); 4. Colossians 2:9-10; 5. Nicene Creed, -AD 325; 6. Arius, letter to Eusebius, bishop of
Nicomedia, -A.D. 319; 7. Apostles' Creed; 8. Wayne Grudem, professor of Theology and
Biblical Studies at Phoenix Seminary, in *Systematic Theology* (Zondervan, 1995).